# THE LITTLE GIRL GOD
# NEVER FORGOT

## A Memoir of Pain, Healing, and Divine
## Restoration

### By:
### Julia A. Hamilton

LCCN: 2026900331

**When the world forgot her, God remembered**


When my father was gone, when my mother was lost,
when my innocence was stolen,

God was still writing my story.

# TRIBUTE PAGE

In Loving Memory of My Parents, my father, who returned to God's arms when I was only two. Though I never knew your voice or your embrace, your absence became the space where God began shaping my strength. My mother, whose battles were heavy and whose struggles I did not fully understand. I thank God for the life you gave me, and I release the rest into His mercy and grace. Today, I honor you both—not through pain, but through the healing God has brought to my heart. May your souls rest in His eternal peace.

# DEDICATION

This book is dedicated to the people who gave my pain purpose and my healing meaning —

My late parents — the two souls whose lives shaped the beginning of my story. Daddy, though you left this world when I was only two, your absence carved a space in me that God Himself chose to fill. Mama, your struggles were heavy, and your journey was complicated, but I honor the life you gave me and the lessons that shaped my strength.

To my daughters, Marika and Darquelle:

You are the reason I kept fighting when life tried to break me. You grew up watching me survive storms you never fully understood, and you still became my most outstanding teachers in strength, love, and forgiveness.

Everything I endured, everything I overcame, everything I became — I did it so you would never have to start where I started.

You are my legacy, my joy, and my reminder that God restores what was once broken.

To my grandchildren Greyson (Peanut), GraceLynn (Butter), and Mariah (Jelly):

You are proof that generational curses end with me. I pray that your lives are filled with love, protection, and safety I never knew as a child. May you grow up covered in the kind of love that heals, strengthens, and elevates. You are my answered prayers, my sunshine, and the reason my story had to change.

To my sisters, Martha, Mary, Annie Laura, Shantell, Sarah, and Elouise:

We did not always have the closeness we deserved, but we all survived a childhood that tried to break us. This book is a reminder that even through pain, distance, trauma, and silence — we are still connected by blood, by resilience, and by God's mercy.

I honor each of you for your own journey, your strength, your scars, and your survival.

We are proof that generational curses can be challenged, confronted, and defeated.

And finally—

To the little girl I used to be:

I wrote this book for you.

I'm sorry you had to carry so much.

But look at us now —

We survived.

We healed.

We overcame.

And now, through God's grace, we are free.

# ACKNOWLEDGEMENTS

Writing this book has been one of the hardest and holiest journeys of my life. There were moments I had to stop, breathe, cry, and pray before I could continue. This book is not just a story — it is healing, a release, and a testimony. And I could not have reached this place alone.

First and foremost, to God:

Thank You for carrying me when I didn't have the strength to carry myself.

Thank You for covering me as a child, comforting me as a woman, and calling me into purpose when the world tried to silence me.

Every chapter of this book exists because of Your grace, Your protection, and Your unfailing love. You never forgot me, even when I felt forgotten. This book is proof of Your faithfulness.

To my daughters:

Thank you for loving me through every season — the broken ones, the growing ones, and the healed ones. You gave me reasons to keep going when giving up felt easier. Your strength, your laughter, your patience, and your presence kept me grounded. Everything I fought through, I fought through for you. You are my heart and my motivation.

To my grandchildren:

Your joy reminds me of why I broke every generational curse that tried to cling to our family.

Thank you for bringing light into my life, for giving me hope, and for showing me what love looks like in its purest form. You are the healed generation I prayed for.

To my sisters:

We survived the same storms in different ways. I appreciate your strength, your resilience, your forgiveness, and your presence.

Even through distance, trauma, and unspoken pain, we remain connected.

Your journeys matter. Your stories matter. You matter.

To every woman who has ever felt invisible, unloved, or unworthy: Thank you for encouraging me without even knowing it. Thank you for reminding me why telling this story was necessary.

You are seen. You are valued. You are loved. My prayer is that this book gives you courage, comfort, and clarity.

To the people who hurt me, abandoned me, or doubted me:

You taught me strength, boundaries, and discernment. You pushed me closer to God.

And for that — unexpectedly — I thank you.

To the readers of this book:

Thank you for holding my story with tenderness. Thank you for giving space to my truth.

Thank you for allowing my healing to meet you on your own journey.

May you find hope in these pages and strength in your own story.

And finally—

To the little girl inside me:

Thank you for surviving long enough for the woman to heal.

Your courage is the reason this book exists.

With love, gratitude, and grace—

Julia

# AUTHOR'S NOTE

If you are holding this book in your hands, I want you to know something from the very beginning:

This was not easy to write. But it was necessary.

Every chapter required me to revisit places I never wanted to return to. Every truth required courage I didn't always feel. Every memory required healing I hadn't fully embraced. But God placed it on my heart to write this — not because my story is perfect, but because someone else needs to know they are not alone.

I didn't write this book to expose my family, or to reopen wounds, or to blame anyone for their own brokenness. I wrote it to honor the girl I used to be, and to encourage the woman who is still becoming.

There were nights I cried while writing. There were mornings I didn't think I had the strength to keep going. There were moments when the enemy whispered, "Who do you think you are to tell this story?" But God whispered louder, "Tell it — someone's healing is attached to your honesty."

If your childhood was painful, you are not alone. If your relationships left scars, you are not alone. If you've struggled with feeling unloved, unworthy, or unwanted, you are not alone. If you've battled low self-esteem or generational pain, you are not alone.

I pray that as you read my story, you will find pieces of your own. I pray that God speaks to you through the lines, the chapters, and the quiet moments in between. I pray you feel hope rising where hurt once lived.

Most of all, I pray you walk away remembering this:

Your story is not over. Your past is not your identity. Your survival is not accidental. And your healing is not impossible.

Thank you for giving me the honor of sharing my heart with you. Thank you for turning these pages with compassion. Thank you for allowing my testimony to speak into your life.

May this book bless you, strengthen you, and remind you that even in the darkest chapters, God is still writing the story.

With love, truth, and gratitude,

Julia A. Hamilton

# SPIRITUAL FOREWORD

People write some stories. Others are written by pain, but this story — this testimony — was written by God.

Before a single chapter existed, before a wound was formed, before a tear ever fell, God had already marked this woman for survival.

Her life was shaped by loss, by trauma, by silence, by secrets, and by storms she never asked for — yet she stands today, not as a victim, but as a vessel.

This book is not just her story; it is evidence of a God who specializes in taking what the enemy meant for destruction and turning it into destiny.

The woman behind these pages grew up in a world that should have broken her.

A father gone too soon. A mother fighting battles beyond her control. Sisters walking through their own unspoken wounds. A childhood covered in shadows instead of safety.

Innocence was stolen. Worth attacked. Self-esteem shattered. Relationships that mirrored pain instead of love.

Yet even in the darkest places, God was present —softly, silently, faithfully.

He was there when she felt alone. He was there when her voice was silent. He was there when her heart was breaking.

He was there when she learned how to survive without guidance. He was there when generational curses tried to claim her life — and He was there when she rose above them.

Her story is not just about survival; it is about spiritual inheritance. It is about breaking chains her mother couldn't break, shattering cycles her sisters learned to endure, and rewriting the future for her daughters and grandchildren.

This book is a holy reminder that nothing — not trauma, not family wounds, not abuse, not abandonment — can cancel the calling God places on a life.

As you read these pages, prepare your heart.

Not just to witness her healing, but to see your own reflection in it.

Her story will touch the abandoned child in you.

It will confront the wounds you buried.

It will speak to the woman who still smiles while silently breaking.

It will remind you that God never leaves, even when everyone else does.

May every chapter lift you.

May every truth free you.

May every revelation remind you that God heals in layers, restores in seasons, and redeems with purpose.

And may you know this:

If God protected her through everything she endured, if He held her through trauma, loss, betrayal, and brokenness, if He lifted her from the lowest places and crowned her with strength — He will do the same for you.

This is not just a book. This is a testimony. A ministry. A healing journey. A spiritual awakening. A declaration that the enemy did not win.

Welcome to a story only God could write — a story that will remind you what grace truly looks like.

# Table of Contents

# PROLOGUE

The Night Everything Changed

I was still a little girl when I first realized the world wasn't safe for me.

I remember the house being too quiet — the kind of silence that makes a child hold her breath without knowing why. I remember walking on tiptoes, afraid to disturb anything, afraid to wake anything, afraid of what might meet me on the other side of a half-closed door. I didn't have the words for it then, but I felt it, the heaviness, the fear, the confusion, the emptiness of growing up in a world that didn't have room to protect me.

I didn't understand why my father wasn't there. I didn't understand why my mother was lost in her own pain. I didn't understand why the people who should have loved me became the ones I learned to fear.

All I knew was that I felt alone.

Alone in my bed.

Alone in that house.

Alone in my own family.

Alone in a life that seemed determined to silence me before I could speak.

There was a night — a night I can still feel more than I can remember — when my childhood ended long before my age ever caught up.

A night when innocence slipped away, replaced by questions no child should ever carry.

A night when darkness didn't just fall around me —it fell on me.

And yet… something else was there too.

A whisper.

A presence.

A feeling I didn't understand at the time.

It wasn't loud.

It wasn't dramatic.

It wasn't even something I could name.


It was simply there —

a quiet awareness that even though I was hurting,

even though I was scared,

even though I felt abandoned,

I was not alone.

Looking back now as a grown woman, I know precisely what that presence was.

It was God.

He was there in the room where my innocence was broken.

He was there in the silence of a house full of people who didn't see me.

He was there when my mother was lost inside her own battles.

He was there when words were spoken over my life that were meant to destroy me.

He was there when I cried with no one to hear me.

He was there when I learned to survive by pretending I didn't hurt.

God was there —

quietly, faithfully, watching over a little girl who thought no one cared.

I didn't know it then, but the night everything changed for me was also the night God decided the story would not end there.

This book begins with a broken little girl, but it does not end with one.

Because the same God who saw me then is the same God who lifted me, healed me, restored me, and turned my deepest wounds into my most incredible testimony.

This is not the story of what happened to me. This is the story of what God brought me through.

# INTRODUCTION

I didn't write this book because I have a perfect story. I wrote it because I survived an imperfect one. For years, I carried pain I never talked about — the kind that sits quietly in your chest, shaping your choices, your relationships, your confidence, and your self-worth.

I learned how to smile through trauma, how to encourage others while I was breaking inside, and how to keep going even when I didn't know what I was moving toward.

I grew up without a father. I watched my mother lose herself to addiction.

I survived abuse, loneliness, and family wounds that most people never see from the outside. I loved men who broke me. I tolerated pain I didn't deserve.

I battled low self-esteem, deep insecurities, and the haunting belief that I wasn't enough.

And for a long time, I thought I was alone, but I wasn't. God was there — in every moment I thought I was forgotten. I wrote this book because somewhere out there is another woman who's still smiling through the pain. Another woman who still feels like the little girl inside her is crying. Another woman who doesn't feel chosen, protected, loved, or worthy.

Another woman whose story looks nothing like what she imagined life would be.

I wrote this book for her. I wrote this book for the generations of women in my family who never had the space to heal, and I wrote it for the little girl I used to be — the one who deserved love, safety, and tenderness long before she ever learned the language of survival.

This is not a story of defeat. It's a story of deliverance. It's a story of what happens when God steps into a life that was supposed to break. It's a story of how pain can become purpose, how trauma can become transformation, and how a broken girl can become a powerful woman of God. If you have ever felt abandoned, overlooked, mistreated, or unworthy, this book is for you. If you have ever stayed in a place that hurt you because leaving felt even scarier, this book is for you. If you have ever struggled to love yourself, this book is for you.

You are not alone.

Your story is not over.

And the pain you survived is not wasted.

My prayer is that as you turn these pages, you will find pieces of yourself, you will feel less alone, and you will hear God's whisper saying:

"You were never forgotten."

This is my truth.

This is my healing.

This is my becoming.

Welcome to my story —and welcome to your own breakthrough.

# CHAPTER 1
# BORN INTO AN EMPTY SPACE

**"When my father and my mother forsake me, then the Lord will take me up."**
**— Psalm 27:10**

## Devotional Reflection:

**Even when I entered this world feeling unseen, God already had His eyes on me. What felt empty to others was never empty to Him — He filled the space with His presence long before I understood it.**

I don't remember my father's voice. I don't remember his face. I don't remember the way he smelled or the way he held me, but I do remember the emptiness.

My father died when I was just two years old, long before I had the language to name loss or the understanding to feel it. Yet somehow, even as a child, I knew something was missing. There was a space in my life — a quiet, aching hole that no one explained, but everyone tiptoed around.

Other children had fathers who showed up at school, who fixed broken toys, who kissed scraped knees, who filled their homes with laughter.

I had a memory that didn't exist. I had a presence that felt more like a shadow than a person.

Growing up without a father didn't just affect my childhood — it shaped my identity.

I learned early that the world could take something from you before you even knew what you had. That loss became the first wound of my life. The beginning of a silent ache I carried for years. The foundation of a story that started with absence, but what I didn't know then was this:

Even in the places where people were missing, God was already present.

# CHAPTER 2
# A MOTHER LOST IN ADDICTION

**My grace is sufficient for you, for My strength is made perfect in weakness."**

**— 2 Corinthians 12:9**

## Devotional Reflection:

**My mother's addiction created wounds I didn't deserve, but God's strength carried me through what her weakness could not. Even in the brokenness, His grace kept building the woman I would one day become.**

My mother loved me — I never doubted that, but addiction loved her too, and it loved her harder.

Alcohol stole parts of her I desperately needed. Some days she was there, talking, laughing, cooking. Other days, she disappeared into a bottle, and I disappeared into myself.

As a child, I didn't understand addiction. I only understood the inconsistency.

I understood fear. I understood the feeling of needing someone who wasn't emotionally available. I learned how to read the tone of her footsteps. I learned how to stay quiet to keep the peace. I learned how to pretend everything was normal so nobody would ask questions.

I had to grow up before childhood truly happened. Most little girls learn to braid hair and play with dolls. I learned how to manage trauma and keep secrets. I learned how to take care of myself because the person responsible for taking care of me was fighting her own battles.

People expected me to become just like her — an alcoholic, unstable, broken.

But what they didn't know was this:

The pain that tried to destroy me was the same pain God used to build me.

# CHAPTER 3
# A CHILD WITHOUT A PLACE TO BELONG

**"God sets the lonely in families."**

**— Psalm 68:6**

## Devotional Reflection:

**Every time I felt displaced, God was quietly preparing a place for me. My belonging was never lost — it was simply waiting for me to grow into it.**

I grew up in a house with siblings, but not with connection. We shared blood, but not a bond.

We shared space, but not closeness. I often felt like a stranger in my own family.

While other kids played together, laughed together, fought together, and protected each other, I watched from a distance. I didn't have a place to run to. I didn't have a sibling to confide in.

I didn't have a built-in friend like most children do. People surrounded me, yet I felt utterly alone. There were holidays when I felt invisible. There were moments when I stood in a room full of family and still felt like I didn't belong to anyone. There were nights when silence hurt more than any words could. This lack of connection shaped me.

It taught me how to be independent — but also how to isolate.

It taught me how to be strong — but also how to hide. It taught me how to survive — but not how to receive love.

It wasn't until adulthood that I realized loneliness isn't the absence of people — it's the absence of connection.

# CHAPTER 4
# VIOLATED INNOCENCE

**"He heals the brokenhearted and binds up their wounds."**

**— Psalm 147:3**

## Devotional Reflection:

**What was taken from me could have destroyed me, but God held the pieces that others shattered. My healing is proof that no wound is too deep for His hands to restore.**

Some pains are too heavy for a child to carry. Some wounds are too deep to put into words.

I was mistreated. I was molested by people who should have protected me. I was violated by those who should have been safe.

I didn't understand it when it happened. I only understood the shame. I understood the confusion.

The fear. The silence.

I learned early that not everyone who says "I love you" means it. I learned that family can hurt you. I learned that trust is not always safe.

The trauma didn't just touch my body — it invaded my spirit, my self-worth, my understanding of love.

For years, I carried blame that wasn't mine. I carried guilt that didn't belong to me. I had scars from wounds I never caused.

But now, as a healed woman, I speak this truth loudly: I was a child.

What happened to me was not my fault, and God never stopped seeing me — even when I was too ashamed to see myself.

# CHAPTER 5
# WORDS THAT WOUNDED THE SOUL

Death and life are in the power of the tongue."

— **Proverbs 18:21**

### Devotional Reflection:

**The words spoken over me tried to shape my destiny, but God whispered a different truth. His voice reminded me that wounds from people do not override the identity He placed inside me.**

Pain doesn't always come from actions — sometimes it comes from words.

And the words spoken over me as a child had the power to shape how I saw myself.

"You'll be nothing."

"You're just like your mother."

"You'll end up drunk."

"You'll never be anything."

"No man will ever want you."

I wasn't just hurt — I was labeled.

Those words stuck to my spirit like tattoos I never asked for. They shaped my self-esteem, my decisions, my relationships, and my sense of self-worth.

When you hear negativity long enough, you start to believe it. You start making choices based on the lies instead of your potential. You begin living beneath your destiny because you've been told you don't deserve more.

But God —God had a different plan for my life.

He allowed the words spoken over me to become fuel instead of failure. He allowed the insults to become motivation. He allowed the cruel predictions to become proof of His power.

Because at 54 years old —

I am not an alcoholic.

I am not a failure.

I am not a statistic.

I am not what they said I would be.

I am who God says I am.

And their words no longer have power over my life.

# CHAPTER 6
# BECOMING THE WOMAN WHO LOVED UNLOVED

*"Love bears all things, believes all things, hopes all things, endures all things."*
*— 1 Corinthians 13:7*

## Devotional Reflection:

**I learned to love from a place of lack, yet God multiplied it into abundance. Loving the unloved became my ministry, not because I had it all, but because I knew what it felt like to have nothing.**

I didn't wake up one day and decide to choose unhealthy love. It started long before I ever knew what a relationship was. When you grow up without affection, without affirmation, without a safe place to land, you enter adulthood with an emptiness so deep that anyone who shows you the slightest attention feels like a blessing.

I didn't know what healthy love looked like, so I confused being chosen with being wanted, and I confused being tolerated with being loved.

The little girl in me — the one who grew up without her father, the one who tiptoed around an alcoholic mother, the one who felt invisible in a house full of siblings — she ran my relationships.

She was still searching for someone to stay, someone to protect her, someone to choose her on purpose.

And because she was aching, I stayed in places where the woman in me was dying, I stayed when I should have left, I loved harder when I should have been healing, I poured into men who didn't have the capacity, the desire, or the intention to pour back into me.

# CHAPTER 7
# THE ABUSE I NEVER THOUGHT
# I'D TOLERATE

"No weapon formed against you shall prosper."

— Isaiah 54:17

## Devotional Reflection:

**What I survived was never meant to destroy me —
and it didn't. God shielded parts of me I didn't even
know needed protecting, preserving the strength I would
need for the chapters ahead.**

Abuse doesn't always show up with bruises. Sometimes
it shows up wearing a charm.

Sometimes it holds your hand and tells you everything
you've been waiting your whole life to hear. Sometimes it
feels like destiny before it reveals itself as destruction.

People love to ask, "Why didn't you just leave?" But they
never ask, "What made you stay?"

They never ask what it feels like to grow up hungry for
love and then meet someone who promises to give you the
world — until they turn around and take your soul.

He didn't hit me on the first day. The first day, he studied me. He learned what I liked and what I feared. He learned the wounds I carried. He learned how badly I wanted to be loved, and he used that knowledge like a weapon.

The abuse came slowly — not like a storm, but like a quiet drizzle that turns into a flood before you even realize you're drowning.

A little control here, a little jealousy there, a little anger, a little silence, a little punishment disguised as "love."

Then one day, the man who once held my face gently in his hands became the man who gripped my wrists until my skin burned.

I tolerated things I swore I'd never tolerate; I blamed myself for his anger, I apologized for his outbursts, and I tried to love him into becoming a better man.

But love doesn't fix someone who isn't trying.

There were moments I didn't even recognize myself. Moments where I felt like I was watching my own life from the outside — watching a woman who deserved the world settle for pain that wasn't hers to carry.

He drained every drop of self-worth I had left, he attacked my looks, he attacked my intelligence, and he attacked my confidence. I began believing him more than I believed in myself.

The worst part? I still hoped he would change, I prayed for him, I cried over him, and I even begged God to save the relationship long after God was trying to save me from it.

My breaking point wasn't loud, it wasn't dramatic, it was a quiet moment where I realized:

If I stay, I will lose myself completely.

Leaving wasn't easy. It took strength I didn't know I had. But the day I walked out of that door, I walked back into myself. God didn't just rescue me. He reintroduced me to the woman I was always meant to be.

And for the first time in a long time, I whispered to myself: "You deserve better. You deserve more. You deserve love that doesn't hurt."

# CHAPTER 8
# THE BATTLE WITH MY OWN REFLECTION

*"I praise You because I am fearfully and wonderfully made."*

— Psalm 139:14

**Devotional Reflection:**

**There were days I could barely recognize the woman in the mirror, but God saw beauty where I saw brokenness. Learning to love myself became an act of worship — a reclaiming of the masterpiece He created.**

Healing doesn't start with leaving the wrong person. It begins with confronting the version of yourself that believed the wrong person was all you deserved.

For years, I looked in the mirror and saw everything people said about me —

not my beauty, not my strength, not my resilience, but every insult, I mean every insult, every wound, every lie that was spoken over my childhood.

I carried low self-esteem like it was a birthright. Like because I didn't have a father, I didn't deserve love, like because my mother was an alcoholic, failure was waiting with my name on it, like the abuse I endured meant something was wrong with me, not the people who hurt me.

I didn't feel pretty enough, I didn't feel smart enough, I didn't feel wanted. Most days, I didn't feel worthy of anything. I smiled in public, but I crumbled in private. I encouraged others, but I couldn't encourage myself. I poured into people, even when I was running on empty.

What I didn't understand back then was simple:

The little girl in me never healed, so the woman in me kept bleeding. I battled thoughts that weren't mine. Thoughts like:

"No one will ever truly love you."

"You're too damaged."

"You're too broken."

"You're not good enough."

"You're not worth choosing."

Those thoughts didn't come from God — they came from a life that taught me to see myself through the eyes of those who mistreated me.

Unhealthy relationships only confirmed what I already believed about myself.

Every time someone rejected me, I heard my childhood; every time someone mistreated me, I felt unworthy again; every time someone left, I felt like a burden.

But somewhere deep inside, God kept whispering: "You are more."

And that whisper grew louder. I started noticing the things I used to ignore — the way I shrunk myself in conversations, the way I accepted less than I deserved, the way I pretended to be okay to keep peace, the way I broke my own heart trying to protect others, the way I lived unloved because I didn't know how to love myself.

The battle with my reflection wasn't about beauty. It was about identity. I had to unlearn the lies.

I had to remind myself of the truth:

I am chosen.

I am seen.

I am enough.

I am deserving.

I am worthy.

I am God's child, not my trauma's leftover.

Healing didn't come overnight.

Some days I felt strong, some days I felt shattered, some days I cried for the little girl who never felt held, but every day, God had me anyway.

The day I started loving myself was the day everything changed.

Not because I felt beautiful — but because I finally understood I didn't have to earn love.

Not from a man, not from my family, not even from myself.

God already loved me deeply, completely, and unconditionally!

And slowly... I began to see the woman He created:

A woman who survived, a woman who healed, a woman who rose, a woman who finally, finally knows her worth.

# CHAPTER 9
# WHEN GOD STEPPED IN

"When the enemy comes in like a flood, the Spirit of the Lord will lift up a standard against him."

— Isaiah 59:19

## Devotional Reflection:

**When life felt overwhelming, God stepped into the places I could no longer carry. His intervention wasn't loud — it was steady, sure, and right on time.**

There were moments in my life when I didn't know how I was still standing.

Moments when the weight of childhood trauma, unhealthy love, loneliness, and emotional wounds felt too heavy to carry. Moments when I struggled to believe I mattered. Moments when I thought the pain would swallow me whole.

But that's the thing about God— He steps in quietly, long before you realize he's already fighting for you. I used to think I survived because I was strong, but looking back now, I know I survived because God refused to let my story end in the same darkness I was born into.

There were nights I cried myself to sleep and somehow woke up with enough strength to face another day. That was God!

Some relationships should have destroyed me, but something in my spirit whispered, "Leave." That was God!

There were moments when I felt unloved, unseen, and unwanted, yet grace kept pulling me through. That was God!

I didn't just walk away from abuse — God carried me out.

He protected me from things I didn't even know were happening, he shielded me from people who meant me harm, he kept my mind when it should have crumbled, he kept my spirit when it should have broken permanently, he kept my purpose alive when life kept trying to bury it.

Even when I doubted myself, even when I accepted less, even when I settled, tolerated, and endured things I shouldn't have…God stayed, God covered, God waited for me to see myself the way he sees me.

There were days when I wanted love so badly, I accepted the counterfeit version, but God loved me enough to remove what I was begging him to fix. He wasn't punishing me — He was protecting me.

I used to ask, "God, why did you let me go through so much? With time, I learned that every wound had a purpose:

The father I never knew taught me to lean on my heavenly Father. The mother lost in addiction

The siblings I never bonded with taught me that family is more than blood — it's love.

The abuse taught me that silence doesn't mean shame — it means survival.

The heartbreak taught me that love doesn't destroy.

The loneliness taught me that being alone with God isn't loneliness — it's preparation.

Every dark season became a piece of the woman I am today.

And then came the shift — not loud, not dramatic, but undeniable. One day, after years of hurting, I felt something I couldn't explain:

Peace. Not temporary peace, not relationship peace, not "things are better today" peace,

but the kind that feels like God Himself laid His hand on your heart and whispered,

"You've suffered enough. Now watch what I do."

That's when everything began to change.

I started seeing myself differently, I started believing that I deserved love that didn't wound me, I started understanding that healing wasn't weakness — it was warfare, I started feeling God's presence more strongly than ever before, and slowly, the little girl inside me — the one who felt forgotten, unwanted, and unworthy — began to heal.

God didn't just step into my story. He rewrote it.

I am not the pain I endured, I am not the lies spoken over my childhood, I am not the mistakes I made while searching for love, I am a testimony, I am a survivor, I am God's reminder that broken beginnings don't prevent beautiful endings.

When I look back now, I don't just see trauma — I see God's fingerprints all over my life.

He was there when I was hurting, he was there when I was confused, he was there when I settled, he was there when I cried, he was there when I walked away, he was there when I decided to choose myself and He is still here, writing chapters I once believed were impossible.

My story isn't just about pain, it's about redemption, it's about deliverance, it's about a God who steps in right before life wins and says, "Not this one. She belongs to Me."

# CHAPTER 10
# BREAKING GENERATIONAL CURSES

"Therefore if the Son sets you free, you shall be free indeed."

— John 8:36

## Devotional Reflection:

**I chose to become the woman who said, "This ends with me." God gave me the authority to break chains that were never meant to follow me into my future.**

People talk about generational curses like they're just habits or patterns, but the truth is, generational curses are spirits, wounds, cycles, and silent agreements passed down through families for years — sometimes centuries.

In my family, the curses were loud and quiet at the same time: loss, abandonment, addiction, brokenness, emotional silence, secrets swept under rugs.

Pain passed from one generation to the next like an inheritance.

My father was gone before I ever knew him. My mother drowned her pain in alcohol.

My siblings and I were raised together, but not raised connected. Nobody talked about healing,

nobody talked about love; nobody talked about trauma. We just survived — the best way we could.

But survival isn't the same as healing. I didn't realize until adulthood that I had inherited more than just a last name —I had inherited wounds I never asked for.

Women in my family learned how to be strong, but not how to be supported, we learned how to give love, but not how to receive it, we learned how to endure pain, but not how to release it, we learned how to keep going, but not how to rest, we learned how to smile, but not how to heal.

I watched addiction steal my mother's life. I watched unhealthy love break the women around me. I watched silence destroy relationships that could have been whole, and for a long time, I feared I was destined for the same things.

People: My own family told me I'd be an alcoholic like my mother. They said I'd be nothing, they said I'd fail, they told the generational story was already written.

But what they didn't know was this: God specializes in rewriting stories everybody else has given up on.

At 54 — I don't drink; I don't smoke.

I didn't become the statistic they tried to tattoo onto my life; I didn't inherit the addictions that ran through my bloodline, I didn't repeat the cycles I was raised in, I didn't become the broken woman my childhood tried to shape me into. I became a cycle breaker.

But breaking generational curses isn't just about what you refuse to do. It's about who you refuse to be. I stopped choosing men who mirrored my childhood trauma, I stopped settling for love that felt like pain, I stopped allowing people to treat me like I was replaceable, I stopped repeating the silence I grew up in, I stopped shrinking to make others comfortable, and I stopped handing down trauma to my children and grandchildren.

Instead, I started giving them things I never had:

Love.

Affection.

Emotional safety.

Encouragement.

Presence.

Protection.

A healed example of what strength looks like.

Breaking curses meant looking at my reflection and saying, "This ends with me."

It meant refusing to numb my pain, it meant facing my trauma head-on, it meant building a life I was never shown, it meant choosing God over generational patterns, and it meant healing from wounds I didn't cause.

Some days were hard. Some days I felt like I was fighting battles from both the past and the present. Some days I questioned if healing was even possible for someone like me — someone with so many scars, but God didn't call me to be a prisoner of my past. He called me to be a deliverer of my bloodline.

And now I realize:

Everything I survived wasn't just for me. It was for the generations after me who will never have to experience the pain I endured.

Because of me, my grandchildren will know love doesn't hurt.

Because of me, my children won't inherit emotional silence.

Because of me, the curse of addiction stops.

Because of me, the cycle of brokenness breaks.

Because of me, the family story changes forever.

I am not my mother's struggle.

I am not my father's absence.

I am not my trauma.

I am not the lie they told me I'd become.

I am the curse breaker.

The story changes.

The generational interrupter.

The woman is rebuilding what was destroyed long before she was born.

And God is using every piece of my pain as the foundation of a legacy I can be proud of.

# CHAPTER 11
# HEALING THE CHILD AND THE WOMAN

**"He restoreth my soul."**

**— Psalm 23:3**

## Devotional Reflection:

**Healing didn't come all at once — it came in layers. God tended to the little girl who was hurting and the grown woman who was still learning to breathe again.**

Healing is never just about the woman you are now. It's about the little girl you once were — the one who learned how to survive long before she ever learned how to live.

For years, I thought healing meant forgetting. I thought it meant pretending the trauma never happened and smiling through the pain and acting like I wasn't affected. Being strong because I had to be, but the truth is, healing doesn't come from ignoring the wound — it comes from acknowledging it.

One day, I realized the woman in me was exhausted, but the little girl inside me was broken.

She was still waiting for someone to protect her. Still waiting for someone to choose her.

Still waiting for someone to say, "What happened to you was wrong." Still waiting to feel safe.

And I had to become that person for her.

Healing required me to go back — not to relive the pain, but to rescue the girl who never got the chance to be free. I told her:

"You did nothing wrong."

"You were never the problem."

"You were never unlovable."

"You didn't deserve what happened to you."

"You were a child — and they failed you."

And with every truth I spoke over her, the woman in me began to heal. I stopped talking to myself like my abusers. I stopped carrying shame that belonged to other people.

I stopped blaming myself for relationships that weren't my responsibility to fix.

I stopped looking at myself through broken mirrors. Healing meant separating every lie from every truth. Healing meant learning that love is not earned — it is given. Healing meant understanding that my worth was never up for debate. Healing meant accepting that the woman I am today has the right to be whole, safe, loved, seen, and valued, but healing wasn't a straight line.

Some days I felt strong. Some days, I felt triggered. Some days, I cried without knowing why.

Some days I wanted to run back to old habits — not because they were good, but because they were familiar.

Healing meant facing loneliness without settling. Healing meant loving myself even when it felt foreign. Healing meant choosing peace over chaos. Healing meant sitting in silence without breaking.

The more I healed, the more I understood something important:

The woman I am now is the answer to the little girl's prayers.

She wanted safety — I gave it to her.

She wanted comfort — I became it.

She wanted love — I learned to love myself.

She wanted someone to protect her — and God made me strong enough to do it.

Healing didn't erase the past, but it freed me from being controlled by it.

And as I healed the child in me, the woman in me rose — wiser, softer, stronger, and finally at peace.

I became whole not because life was perfect, but because I finally permitted myself to let go of the weight that was never mine.

And now…I stand as both:

The child who survived and the woman who refuses to live in survival mode ever again.

# CHAPTER 12
# BECOMING THE WOMAN GOD DESIGNED

**Being confident of this very thing, that He who began a good work in you will complete it…"**

**— Philippians 1:6**

## Devotional Reflection:

**I am not who life tried to make me — I am who God created me to be. His work in me is ongoing, intentional, and unstoppable, and I am finally stepping into the fullness of His design.**

I did not become this woman by accident. I became her because God refused to let my story end where it began. For years, I believed I was broken beyond repair, but God saw a warrior.

I believed I was unlovable, but God saw His daughter. I thought my wounds defined me, but God saw a testimony waiting to happen.

Becoming the woman God designed wasn't about becoming perfect — it was about becoming whole. It meant releasing bitterness. It meant forgiving myself. It meant loving myself the way God always loved me. It meant choosing peace after a lifetime of chaos. It meant recognizing that my survival was not luck — it was destiny.

The woman God designed is not ashamed of her past. She understands it shaped her, but it does not own her. She knows her worth. She knows her calling. She knows her value.

She knows that God turned what was meant to break her into the very thing that made her powerful. I became a woman of:

Strength — because I've been weak before.

Wisdom — because I've lived through mistakes.

Grace — because I've had to forgive people who never apologized.

Faith — because God was the only constant when everything else failed me.

Love — not because it was given to me freely, but because I learned to cultivate it within myself.

The woman God designed walks with her head high — not because life was easy, but because God lifted her when she couldn't lift herself.

She understands that every loss was protection. Every heartbreak was redirection. Every betrayal was clarification. Every closed door was divine intervention.

My life is no longer defined by trauma. It is defined by victory.

I am not the girl they called "nothing". I am not the daughter of addiction. I am not the child of abandonment. I am not the mistakes of broken relationships. I am not the curse they predicted.

I am God's creation — restored, redeemed, and rising. Becoming the woman God designed means I finally see myself through His eyes:

Loved.

Chosen.

Set apart.

Enough.

More than enough.

Strong.

Capable.

Protected.

Destined.

Anointed.

My ending will not resemble my beginning. My story will inspire the very people who doubted I would make it. My voice will break chains for others. My pain will become someone else's hope.

My survival will become a blueprint for healing.

I have become the woman my childhood never imagined —and the woman my future always needed and now, I no longer question who I am. I walk into it.

I am healed.

I am whole.

I am chosen.

I am loved.

I am free.

I am becoming — every single day — exactly who God always designed me to be.

# ABOUT THE AUTHOR

Julia Hamilton is a woman shaped by resilience, strengthened by faith, and transformed by the grace of God. Born into a childhood defined by loss, trauma, and emotional abandonment, she rose from circumstances meant to break her. She turned her story into a testimony of healing, courage, and spiritual renewal.

For decades, Julia carried wounds that no one could see — growing up without her father, surviving her mother's addiction, enduring childhood mistreatment, navigating broken relationships, and battling low self-esteem. Yet through every painful chapter, God's hand was quietly guiding her toward restoration.

Today, Julia is a mother, grandmother, sister, and advocate for emotional and spiritual healing. She is known for her strength, her honesty, her compassion, and her ability to encourage others even while fighting her own battles. Throughout her life, she has used her experiences to inspire, uplift, and support those who feel unseen or forgotten.

With a heart for people and a passion for healing, Julia has dedicated her life to breaking generational curses, rebuilding her sense of worth, and walking boldly in the purpose God designed uniquely for her. Her story is not one of victimhood — it is one of triumph, redemption, and unshakable faith.

The Little Girl God Never Forgot is her first published work, a memoir that pulls back the curtain on pain while shining a bright light on God's power to restore. Julia hopes that through her words, readers will find comfort, courage, and the reminder that no matter how broken your beginning may be, God can rewrite your ending.

Julia resides in the United States, where she continues to inspire others with her faith, wisdom, honesty, and healing journey.

# A CHILDHOOD SCENE

I remember standing on the playground when someone asked about my mom.

It was one of those questions' kids ask without thinking — simple, curious, careless.

"Where's your mom?"

The sun was bright. Kids were laughing. Swings were squeaking back and forth. Everything around me felt normal, but something tight wrapped itself around my chest. My heart started beating fast, like it was trying to warn me.

I thought about my mother the way other kids didn't have to.

About the smell of alcohol.

About the way she sometimes slurred her words.

About the looks from adults.

About the questions, I didn't know how to answer.

I didn't want to explain any of that.

I didn't want to see their faces change.

I didn't want the pity.

I didn't want the judgment.

I didn't want to feel different — again.

So I said it quickly, like ripping off a bandage.

"She's dead."

The words fell out of my mouth and hit the ground between us. No one questioned it. No one asked more. They just nodded and moved on, running back to their games.

I stood there, still.

My stomach twisted, but at the same time, I felt relief.

Relief that I didn't have to explain.

Relief that I didn't have to defend her.

Relief that I didn't have to carry the weight of her addiction out loud.

At that age, I didn't know the word alcoholic.

I only knew embarrassment.

I only knew shame.

I only knew that telling the truth felt heavier than lying.

So I chose the lie that hurt less.

I didn't understand then that I wasn't ashamed of my mother —

I was ashamed of the pain I didn't know how to carry.

I wasn't trying to erase her.

I was trying to protect myself.

And today, when I look back at that little girl on the playground, I don't see a liar.

I see a child trying to survive something she was never meant to carry alone.

# QUESTIONS TO REFLECT ON

Take your time with these questions. You do not need to answer them all at once. Sit with them, pray over them, journal through them, or return to them as God reveals more of your heart.

1. What parts of my childhood have I never allowed myself to grieve?

_____

_____

_____

_____

_____

_____

_____

_____

2. In what ways has my past shaped how I see myself today?

_____

_____

_____

_____

_____

_____

_____

_____

_____

_____

_____

3. Are there wounds I have minimized because I thought I had to "be strong"?

_____

_____

_____

_____

_____

_____

_____

_____

_____

_____

4. What lies about myself did I learn early in life, and where did they come from?

---

---

---

---

---

---

---

---

---

---

---

5. How have my relationships reflected unresolved pain or unmet needs?

_____

_____

_____

_____

_____

_____

_____

_____

_____

_____

_____

6. What patterns do I see repeating in my life that may need healing?

_____

_____

_____

_____

_____

_____

_____

_____

_____

_____

_____

7. Where do I struggle most with feeling loved, chosen, or valued?

_____

_____

_____

_____

_____

_____

_____

_____

_____

_____

8. What would it look like to invite God into the places I avoid?

_____

_____

_____

_____

_____

_____

_____

_____

_____

_____

_____

9. Are there parts of my story I still believe disqualify me from love or purpose?

_____

_____

_____

_____

_____

_____

_____

_____

_____

_____

10. How has God protected me, even when I didn't recognize it at the time?

_____

_____

_____

_____

_____

_____

_____

_____

_____

_____

_____

11. What generational patterns am I being called to break?

_____

_____

_____

_____

_____

_____

_____

_____

_____

_____

_____

12. Who benefits from my healing—children, grandchildren, relationships, or future generations?

_____

_____

_____

_____

_____

_____

_____

_____

_____

_____

_____

13. What does forgiveness mean for me, and what does it not mean?

_____

_____

_____

_____

_____

_____

_____

_____

_____

_____

_____

14. How can I begin to show myself the compassion I freely give to others?

_____

_____

_____

_____

_____

_____

_____

_____

_____

_____

_____

15. What would healing look like if I believed it was truly possible?

_____

_____

_____

_____

_____

_____

_____

_____

_____

_____

# HEALING EXERCISES

These exercises are gentle invitations, not demands. Move at your own pace. Pause when you need to. Invite God into each step.

1. Letter to the Child I Was

Write a letter to your younger self—the age when you felt most alone. Tell her what she needed to hear. Affirm her worth. Acknowledge what she survived. End the letter by reminding her she is safe now.

2. Naming the Wounds

In a journal, list the hurts that still surface in your thoughts or relationships. Next to each wound, write how it has affected your choices. Then write a prayer releasing that wound to God.

_____

_____

_____

_____

_____

_____

_____

_____

_____

3. Rewriting the Lies

List the negative beliefs you learned about yourself (for example: "I'm not enough"). Across from each lie, write God's truth as you now understand it. Read the truths aloud.

_____

_____

_____

_____

_____

_____

_____

_____

_____

_____

## 4. Body Check-In Prayer

Sit quietly. Take slow breaths. Ask God to show you where your body holds tension or pain. Place a hand there and pray for peace, release, and comfort.

_____

_____

_____

_____

_____

_____

_____

_____

_____

_____

5. Forgiveness Without Excusing

Write the names of people who hurt you. Under each name, write what you are choosing to forgive—not to excuse their actions, but to free your own heart. End with a prayer for boundaries and peace.

_____

_____

_____

_____

_____

_____

_____

_____

_____

6. Creating Safe Boundaries

Write down three boundaries you need in order to feel emotionally or spiritually safe. Pray for the courage to honor them.

_____

_____

_____

_____

_____

_____

_____

_____

_____

_____

7. Gratitude for Survival

List five ways God protected or carried you through difficult seasons. Thank Him for each one, even if you didn't recognize it at the time.

_____

_____

_____

_____

_____

_____

_____

_____

_____

_____

## 8. Vision of Wholeness

Describe what a healed version of you looks like—how you speak, love, rest, and trust. Ask God to help you move toward that vision one step at a time.

_____

_____

_____

_____

_____

_____

_____

_____

_____

# AFFIRMATIONS FOR HEALING AND WHOLENESS

Read these affirmations slowly. Speak them out loud if you can. Return to them on hard days. Let them replace the lies with truth.

• I am loved, seen, and remembered by God.

_____

_____

_____

_____

_____

_____

_____

_____

• My past does not define my worth or my future.

_____

_____

_____

_____

_____

_____

_____

_____

_____

_____

_____

_____

• What happened to me was not my fault.

_____

_____

_____

_____

_____

_____

_____

_____

_____

_____

_____

• I am allowed to heal at my own pace.

_____

_____

_____

_____

_____

_____

_____

_____

_____

_____

_____

• I am not broken—I am becoming whole.

• God was with me then, and He is with me now.

_____

_____

_____

_____

_____

_____

_____

_____

_____

_____

_____

• I release shame that does not belong to me.

_____

_____

_____

_____

_____

_____

_____

_____

_____

_____

_____

• I deserve love that feels safe and honoring.

_____

_____

_____

_____

_____

_____

_____

_____

_____

_____

_____

• I am allowed to set boundaries without guilt.

• I am more than what I survived.

_____

_____

_____

_____

_____

_____

_____

_____

_____

_____

• Generational pain stops with me.

• I am worthy of peace, rest, and joy.

_____

_____

_____

_____

_____

_____

_____

_____

_____

_____

• God is restoring what trauma tried to steal.

_____

_____

_____

_____

_____

_____

_____

_____

_____

_____

_____

_____

• I am growing stronger, softer, and wiser.

_____

_____

_____

_____

_____

_____

_____

_____

_____

_____

• I trust God with the parts of my story I still don't understand.

_____

_____

_____

_____

_____

_____

_____

_____

_____

_____

_____

# A SHORT PRAYER

God,

Thank You for walking with me through every chapter of my life—the painful ones and the healing ones. Thank You for never leaving me, even when I felt alone or forgotten. I place my past, my pain, and my healing in Your hands. Help me continue to grow, forgive, and trust You one step at a time. Restore what was broken, strengthen what is healing, and guide me forward in peace.

Amen.

# FINAL BLESSING

May you walk forward knowing you are deeply loved, fully seen, and never forgotten by God. May peace settle where pain once lived, and may hope rise where fear once stood. May God heal what still aches, strengthen what is still growing, and cover you with grace in every season ahead. May your story continue to unfold with purpose, courage, and quiet joy.

Amen

# A MESSAGE TO THE READER

If you have made it this far, I want you to pause for a moment and take a breath. This book asked you to sit with hard truths, tender memories, and quiet places of the heart. Thank you for trusting me with your time, your emotions, and your story as it unfolded alongside mine.

If parts of this book stirred pain, tears, or memories you have kept buried, please know that you are not weak for feeling them—you are human. Healing is not a straight path, and it does not require perfection. It only requires honesty, courage, and time.

My hope is that these pages reminded you that you are not alone, that what happened to you was not your fault, and that your life still holds purpose and promise. No matter where you are in your journey, God sees you, walks with you, and has not forgotten you.

May you close this book with a little more compassion for yourself, a little more hope for tomorrow, and the quiet assurance that healing is possible—one step, one prayer, one day at a time.

With love and gratitude,

Julia A. Hamilton

# ENCOURAGEMENT FOR YOUR OWN JOURNEY

As you continue on your own path, remember this: healing does not mean forgetting, and strength does not mean never hurting. It means choosing yourself even when it feels uncomfortable. It means allowing God to meet you exactly where you are, not where you think you should be.

There may be days when progress feels slow or invisible. On those days, be gentle with yourself. Growth often happens quietly, beneath the surface, long before it is seen on the outside.

You are allowed to rest. You are allowed to say no. You are allowed to set boundaries. You are permitted to hope again.

Trust that God is still working in your life, even in the unanswered questions and the unfinished places. What feels broken today may be the very place where healing is taking root.

Keep going. Your story is still unfolding, and it is worthy of patience, grace, and love.

# HOW I MAINTAIN HEALING

Healing is not something I completed once and never revisited. It is something I choose, gently and intentionally, again and again. Maintaining healing looks different in every season, but these practices help me stay grounded and whole.

I stay honest with myself. When old feelings surface, I acknowledge them instead of judging myself for having them. I remind myself that emotions are information, not failure.

I protect my peace with boundaries. I no longer explain my boundaries to people who benefit from me having none. Peace is not selfish—it is necessary.

I stay connected to God daily. Through prayer, quiet moments, worship, or simply talking to Him throughout the day, I invite God into my thoughts, decisions, and healing.

I choose rest without guilt. Rest is not weakness. It is restoration. I listen to my body and my spirit when they ask me to slow down.

I speak truth when lies return. When old voices try to tell me who I am not, I replace them with God's truth and the affirmations I have learned to believe.

I ask for help when I need it. Healing does not mean doing everything alone. I allow safe people, counselors, and trusted support to walk with me.

I give myself grace. Healing is not linear. Some days are easier than others, and that is okay. I honor progress, not perfection.

Maintaining healing means choosing myself, trusting God, and remembering that I am worthy of the peace I have worked so hard to find.

WHERE I AM NOW

Today, I am not who I used to be—and I am no longer trying to become her again. I live with greater awareness, deeper compassion, and a peace that once felt impossible. I still have memories, but they no longer control my choices. I still feel emotions, but they no longer define my worth.

I am learning to enjoy the quiet moments without fear. I trust my voice. I listen to my body. I honor my needs. I choose relationships that feel safe, honest, and respectful. I walk away from what costs me my peace.

My faith is steadier now—not perfect, but rooted. I no longer rush healing or question God's timing the way I once did. I understand that growth happens in layers, and I permit myself to keep unfolding.

Where I am now is not an ending—it is a place of stability, clarity, and hope. I am grounded. I am becoming. I am grateful. And I am walking forward with courage, trusting that God will continue to guide each step.

*There's beauty in pausing for a moment to reflect.*

www.ingramcontent.com/pod-product-compliance
Lightning Source LLC
Chambersburg PA
CBHW042316120626
46547CB00022B/2351